Photoshop for Photographers

Table of Contents

Disclaimer

While the author has taken the utmost effort to ensure the accuracy of the written content, all readers are advised to follow information mentioned herein at their own risk. The author cannot be held responsible for any personal or commercial damage caused by information. All readers are encouraged to seek professional advice when needed.

About The Author

John Slavio is a programmer who is passionate about the reach of the internet and the interaction of the internet with daily devices. He has automated several home devices to make them 'smart' and connect them to high speed internet. His passions involve computer security, iOT, hardware programming and blogging. Below is a list of his books: John Slavio Special

Introduction

Photographs have been in fashion since they were known to the common man. People use photographs to capture and store their special moments. These photos help them in reliving those precious moments that they spent with their loved ones, friends, or family. But, it is not the 1940s or 1980s now. With time, people have developed various methods of processing images. Today, they capture images not only to remember their moments, but to share them with people on social media platforms like Instagram, Pinterest, Facbook, Twitter, and many others.

In my opinion, this is the very first reason today that almost all the gadgets are equipped with an in-built camera, and big brands like Apple, Samsung, etc., are competing with each other in terms of the camera quality for capturing images and videos. Thanks to these companies, today, almost everyone has a camera of their own, which was not possible a decade ago. However, having a camera does not make you a photographer.

Shooting random images or taking 'selfies' is very different from actual photography. You have to take care of various factors in photography which you don't even think about while taking a selfie. Photography is an art, a science and a process of creating amazing images using a digital device to record light.

The definition itself may sound confusing to some people who are new to photography. In this book, I am going to share various tips and tricks related to photography that you can use to capture various moments at different places with ease. All the tips that I will discuss in this book are based on my personal experience, and I believe that these will help you as much as they have helped me.

Capturing amazing images with the help of your camera is not enough. You need to produce some appealing images from those digital copies of yours as well. If you spend more than 30 seconds studying an image that you took, you will often notice that something is not presented the way you wanted it to be. You can always open such images in Photoshop to correct them and artificially improve them to make them better looking. Once you are done with the photography lessons in this book, you will continue learning about Photoshop and how you can use the same to make your images WOW!

Finally, I want to congratulate you for your purchase of this amazing book. If you follow this book properly, then you will certainly get a lot of value out of it as most of my other readers already have. So, let us start by learning about Photography.

The Basics of Photography for Beginners

Okay, as I have told you earlier in the introduction chapter, the definition that I provided for photography can be confusing for some people. Keeping this in mind, I am going to tell you about photography from scratch.

Photography has really evolved with time and so have the terms related to it. Now, you do not need to remember all the terms and learn them by heart to become a good photographer. There are only a few basic terms that you will need to remember and understand to proceed with photography and this book. So, let us learn these terms –

Aperture

This might be the very first term that you will hear from a photographer, and this is why you should understand it at the beginning. In simple words, an aperture is known as the size of the opening of your camera lens. This is normally used to vary the amount of light in your image. If you think of the aperture as a window, then you can relate them easily. A big window will allow more sunlight to enter your room when compared to a smaller window in the same place. Aperture works in the same way by varying the size of your lens. An aperture which is opened widely will make your photos bright. Similarly, the smaller aperture will make your photos dark. Besides the amount of light, the aperture also influences the sharpness of your image. If the aperture of your camera is wide, then the background will be unfocused while a smaller aperture will give a comparatively sharper image.

Focus

This is another most common term among photographers. Focus is also another factor which affects the sharpness of your image. You can relate the focus of a camera with the focus of your eye. When your eye focuses on an object, then all the objects which are kept in that object tend to be blurry. You can check this by placing your palm in front of you and then focusing on it with your eyes. The focus of your camera works in the same way. All the objects which are in focus of your camera will be sharp, while the objects which fall outside the focus of your camera will be blurry. Today, all cameras are equipped with multi-focus, which allows you to focus on various images at the same time when capturing a photo.

Continuous Focus

You must be familiar with the autofocus function of your smartphone camera. It autofocuses on an object and continues to do so till you take the picture. However, there is a limitation to this function. If the object that you are currently focusing on, using the autofocus feature, starts to move; then the object will go out of focus. This is where the Continuous Focus option comes into play. With this option, your camera will continue to focus on the object, even if it is moving, until you click the image. Hence, helping you to get the sharp image that you desired.

Depth of Focus

Another important term related to focus. It is related to how much of the image is in focus, which is decided by the distance between the furthest and the closest object in the image. This distance is known as the depth of focus.

For landscapes, the depth of focus distance is large. As a result of this, most of the images taken in landscape are in the focus of your camera. The portrait, on the other hand, has a shallow depth of focus, which makes the image looks soft rather than sharp.

Aspect Ratio

You must be familiar with this term as well; if not from your camera, then from the video player on your laptop or smartphone. Aspect ratio fits the video to the screen as per the ratio that you selected on your device. Aspect ratio is an important term related to photography and is often taken into account when printing the images that you captured. It is simply a ratio of height to width. Setting a proper aspect ratio for your image is really necessary to avoid the cropping of the image that occurs when you print it.

Burst Mode

This is one of the most amazing features and one of my favorite as well. If you want to take several images at once, then what you can do is keep clicking the images one by one with your camera until your collection is formed. Alternatively, you can use the burst mode of your camera. When you turn this mode ON, your camera will keep taking the images continuously while you are holding the image button down. How fast your camera takes these images depends on its speed. Some cameras are faster while others are slower. But still, it is the fastest method on your camera to take several pictures in a short time.

Bokeh

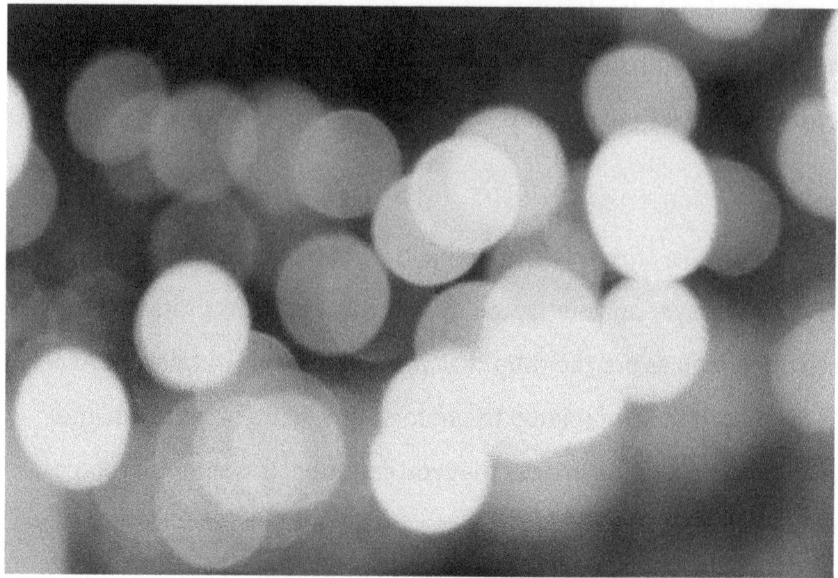

You must have seen this image or an image similar to this one on the internet. This kind of effect is produced with the help of light. Bokeh is the spherical shape created by light sources when they are kept out of focus in an image. This is achieved by widening the aperture of your camera. This is one of the most loved and neatest background effects used by photographers in their work.

Exposure

Exposure is a term related to image effects. Exposure means how light or dark your image is. An image is said to be a perfect one when the amount of light used is adequate. If the light is low in the image, then the image is termed as underexposed. When the light in the image is too much, then it is known as overexposed. I have already told you about aperture, which controls the amount of light in the image. Other important factors which decide the amount of exposure in an image are ISO and shutter speed. Let us now discuss these two terms.

ISO

ISO is the term which is given importance by professionals when they are deciding the exposure of light in their work. ISO decides how sensitive your camera is towards the light. You can change the ISO from the light sensor or simply the sensor option. This option is provided in the camera by default. A low value of ISO means that the camera is not very sensitive to the light. This kind of setting is used by professionals when they are taking an image in daylight. On the other hand, a higher value of ISO means that the camera is very sensitive to the light. This kind of setting is used by professionals when they are taking an image in an environment with low light. ISO needs to be configured properly when you are using your camera in low light; as using an ISO value which is too low can make your image look grainy. To prevent this, the ISO settings are always mixed with aperture and shutter speed to get the perfect exposure of the image.

Shutter Speed

Before discussing the shutter speed, let us first understand what a shutter is. A shutter is the part of your camera which opens and closes to let light get in, in order for you to take a picture. The speed in which the shutter opens and closes during this process is known as the shutter speed. The longer the shutter is opened, the more light will flow in, and vice versa.

Long Exposure

This is another term related to shutter speed and exposure. In this technique, the shutter of the camera is kept open for a longer duration; which helps you get a perfect low light image in an artistic way. This technique is often used by professionals during the night time to take amazing artistic images of the stars.

White Balance

This is **one of the most important terms** related to photography. When the light is low or high, your eye is able to adjust automatically to it. Your camera, on the other hand, cannot do this automatically. This is the reason why your images sometimes turn out to be a bit yellow or blue. To correct this and to take photos like a pro, you need to use the proper white balance in your images. Using the appropriate white balance value will make all the white objects appear white in the photos as well. You can use the automatic option for white balance which is present in cameras today. But, this option is not very accurate. Based on my own experience in photography, I advise you to adjust this setting manually.

Rule of Thirds

This is the most well-known rule of photography. I do not know a single professional who does not know this rule and does not use it in their work. Why does every professional use this rule in their work? They use it because this rule works every time and helps them to capture professional images with minimum effort. If you are really serious about capturing images like a pro and you have very little knowledge about photography, then you should learn this rule by heart and implement it in your work. The basic idea behind the rule of thirds is to imagine the image that you see through your camera in 3 boxes, both vertically and horizontally, so that you have a total of 9 parts of your image. Now, place the point of interest of your image (that is the part of the image that you want to draw attention to) at the intersection point of the lines which are dividing your image horizontally and vertically into 9 parts. If you do this, then your image will be more balanced, and more the viewer will be able to interact more easily and vividly with your image.

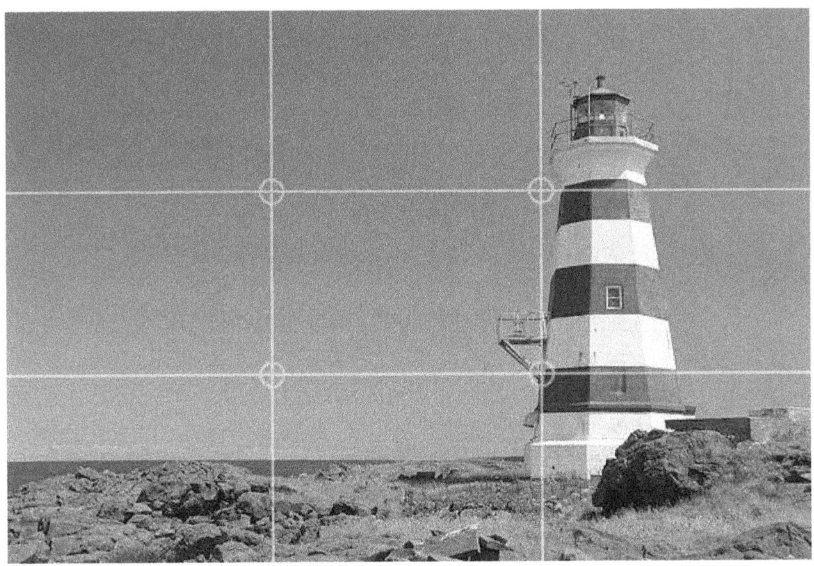

So, that's it with the basics of the camera. If you understood the terms, then I highly recommend you to go and practice these with your camera to polish your photography skills. If you followed this chapter correctly, then you should have already seen improvement in your skills. In the next chapter, I will tell you about various other tricks that you can use to capture professional looking images with ease.

Tips & Tricks for Capturing Images Like Professionals

Okay, in this chapter, you will learn various tricks that I personally use to take amazing images. I am no professional but even so, most of my images are pretty decent. These tricks have helped me a lot, and they will help you as well; providing you follow this chapter thoroughly. So, without wasting any more time, let us begin with the tricks for awesome photography.

Never Underestimate the Manual Focus

Yes, I agree that we are living in the technology era and that people today trust the use of technology in their work more than anything else. But I still recommend that you use manual focusing instead of the automatic focusing when taking a photo with your camera. This is because; no matter how smart your camera is, its judgment of focus can never be fully accurate; especially in low light. Your camera will always struggle with focusing when you are taking a picture in the dark. Manual focusing, on the other hand, is an easy way out of this situation and plus; it is faster than automatic focusing. Let us take an example to understand more about manual focusing. Take a situation where you are taking an image of some birds sitting on the branches of a tree. In this case, your camera will mainly focus on the branches of the tree. Manual focusing, on the other hand, will allow you to have better control over your work in such situations.

The Half Shutter Method

If you like prefer using automatic focus, then make sure you do it right. Most newbies are unaware of the proper use of the shutter button. They think that the shutter button is only there for taking the image. **NO**, the shutter button works in two ways. If you press the shutter button to half, then your camera will lock all the settings, including the focus on the object. Once it locks it down, you will see a green signal or will hear a beep sound. This is to inform you that all the settings have been locked and you can now take the picture. Then you should press the shutter button completely to capture an image. In case, you did not hear any such beep sound or did not see a green signal after pressing the shutter button to half; then it means that your settings were not locked by your camera and you should re-take it.

Throw Your Glasses Away While Photographing

Wearing glasses can sometimes turn out to be irritating and can also prevent you from capturing the perfect image. So, would it be worse to not use them while photographing? Yes, it is true. You can capture amazing images without wearing your eyeglasses. Every camera today has a small knob near the viewfinder of the camera. This knob is known as diopter adjustment knob. With the help of this knob, you can set the value of your eyeglasses in your camera and then can use it to capture the best shot.

Use Custom Settings to Save Time

If you use your camera to take images in the same environment and conditions, then you can set up the best settings and then save them in the custom settings of your camera. Every camera today has a custom setting option enabled. This will help you in taking professional images faster. For example, let us say that you take images of people in the same room every day with the same light amount. Then, instead of setting everything to the appropriate levels every time you take an image, you can set the settings once in your camera and can save them. You can then recall these settings with a click when you are ready to take another image.

Stick with sRGB Color Mode

sRGB is known as the standard color mode and is used in all digital works, including digital images, the internet, and printing. By default, your camera shoots in sRGB mode. However, there is another color mode which is known as Adobe RGB. This color mode has a larger color range than the standard sRGB mode, which influences the newbies to use it. However, no daily life gadget will show you the colors that will be recorded using the Adobe RGB mode. So, why would you even want to use them? I highly advise you to stick to sRGB when you are taking images.

Keep Your Camera Up to Date

Almost all the cameras that are available in the market today receive a frequent update from their respective companies to eliminate some errors which may be conflicting with the photo quality. Hence, it is always recommended to keep your camera's firmware up to date.

Use Fast Memory Cards

If you are a fan of the burst mode, then you should use a fast memory card in your camera. A fast memory card makes your camera's processing a lot faster than before; which improves the results of the burst mode. Most people today use a class 4 memory card. However, I personally use a class 10 memory card in my camera, and I recommend you to use the same. Many leading memory card developing companies, like San Disk, have developed even faster memory cards then class 10. Get those if you can. Just remember, the higher the class of your memory card is, the better the processing time.

Control the Camera Flash

Most of the cameras today have an inbuilt flash for photography. Although it is a good thing, using flash can damage the image quality by building harsh shadows, and that is why I recommend that you use a flash diffuser. The diffuser will soften the harsh flash light to help you take images professionally. If you do not have a flash diffuser with you, then you can simply cover the flash with a tissue paper (white in color). That will work pretty well.

Never Forget the Lens Hoods

Another common mistake among newbies today is that they ignore the use of a lens hood while taking a picture. I highly recommend you to use the lens hoods in your photography. It not only prevents your lens from the damage that can occur from the bumps, but it also eliminates the lens flare, hence improving the image quality to a certain level.

Always Use a Grip

There are times when you will have to use the longer lens in your work. In such cases, you should always use a camera grip to balance the weight of your camera. Moreover, whether you use a longer lens or not, using a grip is always known to improve the image quality in portrait mode, so why ignore them at all?

Use the Auto Distortion Correction Tool

As the name suggests, this tool helps in correcting the distortion automatically. Various lens kits which are available today have some kind of distortion because of the optical elements. This distortion can be easily eliminated using the auto distortion correction tool. Almost all cameras have this feature today. If you are about to buy a camera, then I recommend that you check the gadget for this feature.

Use Slow Sync for Better Exposure

If you take images in the darkness, then you may sometimes find yourself in a situation where the object that you are focusing on has appropriate light while the background remains the dark. In such cases, you can use the Slow Sync feature which is available in the flash menu of your camera. When you turn this feature ON, then your camera takes two exposures which are then blended together to present you the final image. It is recommended to keep your camera still while using this feature.

Take Care of the Sensor

Always keep your camera's sensor clean and free from any kind of dirt and dust. If you do not do so, then you will see some particles in your images because of the dust present on your sensor. You can also clean your sensor yourself. if you are unsure about it, then I recommend you to go to a professional to get it cleaned.

Never Underestimate the Histogram

Being able to know the exposure quality of your image is one of the best features of digital cameras today. However, some of the newbies and even professionals ignore the use of the histogram. As soon as you click an image, you can view it instantly with histograms to check the exposure. Most of the cameras today have a total of 4 histograms to tell the photographer if their image is underexposed, overexposed, or well exposed.

Now, it is time for you to pick up your camera and try these new tips and tricks yourself. Speaking of amazing images, one term that strikes my mind is perspective. We all know what perspective is, however, in photography we use forced perspective to generate amazing images. I will tell you more about forced perspective in the next chapter of this book.

Perspective Tricks to Shoot Images Like a Pro!

Okay, so let us start by understanding what forced perspective really is. It is a primary photography technique which is used by professionals all over the world to generate illusion in their work. This illusion is applied to make objects small or large in their photography. When used correctly, the concept of distance also becomes fun and easy with forced perspective. The forced perspective is used to create effects which are logically impossible in actual life. For example, showing one person in a gigantic shape in the image. Let us learn a few perspective tricks that will help you to shoot images like a pro! These tricks can also be used to create videos with amazing perspective effects. So, let us start!

Understand the Importance

Usually, people either give importance to what is in the background, or to what is in the front of it. In forced perspective, if you will have to give importance to the both of these equally. Giving equal importance to objects of different sizes is the first priority of creating illusions.

The Position of the Objects Matter

Where you keep your objects matters a lot when creating illusions. If you place your objects to the last column of the Rule of Third, then your image will be more balanced and more appealing in creating illusions. Take a look at the image below for example.

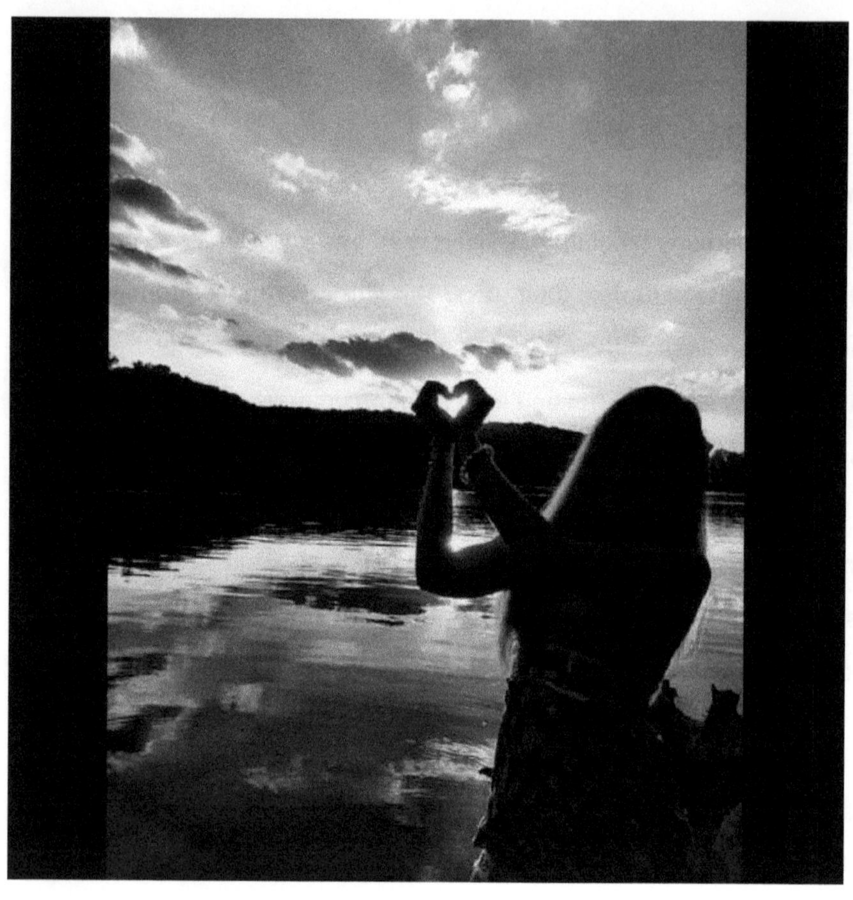

Using Zoom to Connect the Images

It is highly recommended to use Zoom to connect the objects in the images together. If you work in high zoom, then you can easily connect different objects in your image together as you will have more freedom to do so to get better results. Doing so will also give you more freedom in creating the size illusion when clicking the image from your normal eye level. Take the below image as an example.

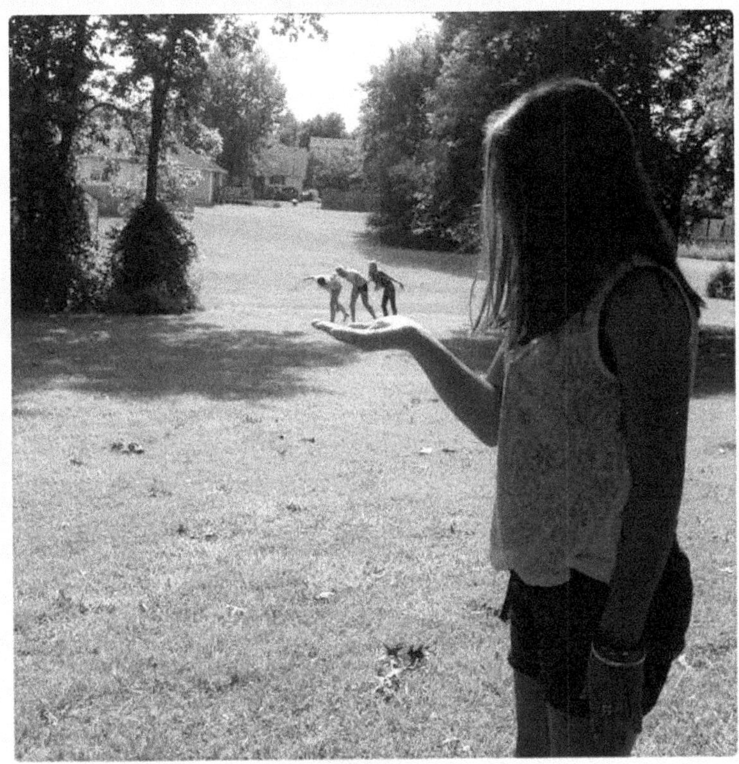

Play with Point of View

Depending on how you use the point of view, the objects in your images can be changed to small or large length. For example, if you are closer to one object than the other, then the first object will appear larger compared to the second. Also, there will be a big variation in the length of the objects based on the height at which you capture the image. If the height of your point of view is less than the height of the object, then the object will appear large in your image. Similarly, if the point of view of your camera is placed at a height greater than your object, then the object will appear to be small in height. Below is an example for the same to help you understand better. In this example, the object seems greater than its actual height and also larger than the man.

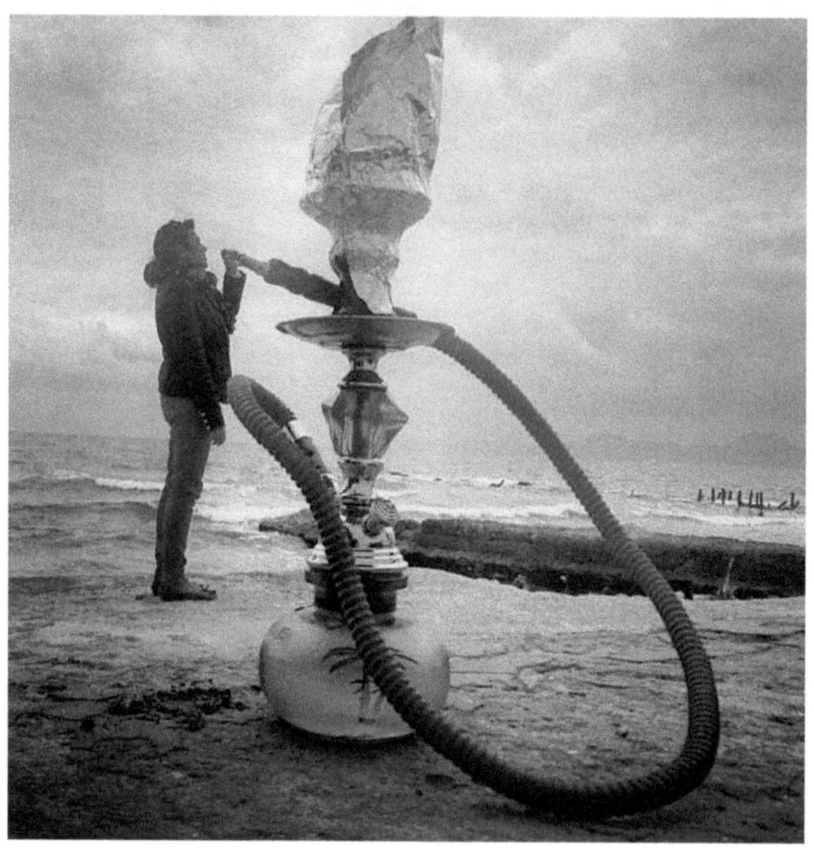

Focus is the Evergreen Element

It does not matter if you are using the forced perspective tricks or are simply capturing an image, the focus always matters. However, it matters a little more than usual when we are using it to apply the forced perspective in our images. Most beginners take images applying the forced perspective which seem fake. Why? Because they simply ignore the concept of using focus in forced perspective. Based on my own experience, I recommend you to use focus in all your perspective illusions. You will have to take care that the focus on both the objects of your image, with whom you are creating an illusion, is equal. If the lighting of the objects is not same, then your work will start looking fake. Always remember that a perfect illusion is the one which succeeds in fooling the human eye to believe what is in the image.

Here is an example of the use of perfect focus to correct the light exposure of the objects while creating a perfect illusion.

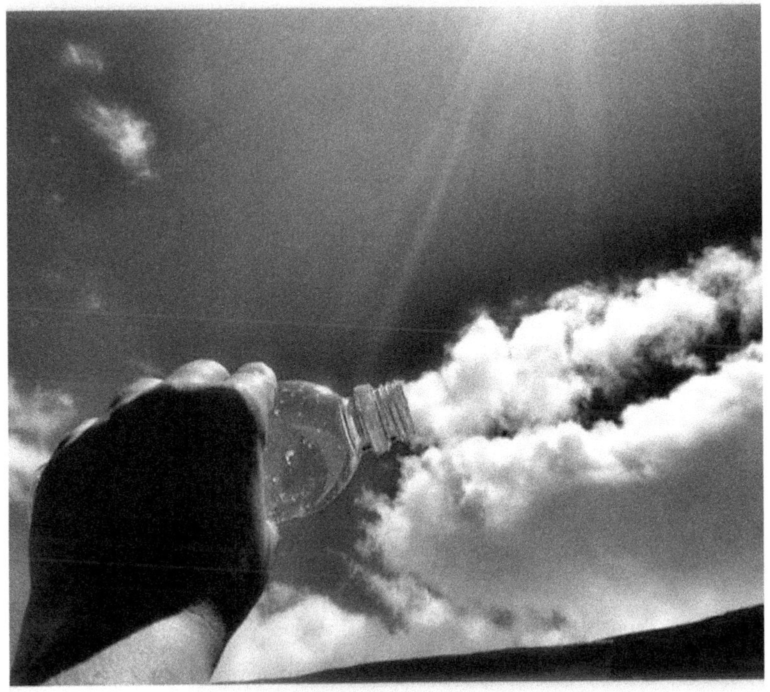

So, how well did you understand the concept of forced perspective and how to use it in your work to look like a pro? Do not know yet? Then it is time for you to go out and use it in your work. The more you practice, the better you understand, and better your work will be. In the next chapter of this book, I will tell you how you can use the various kind of filters to add artificial effects in your images.

Using Filters to Shoot Images Like a Pro!

I do not know a single professional who will not play with artificial effects to create amazing images. All photographers use some sort of filter in their work to create artificial special effects to make their work unique and more appealing to the viewers. In this chapter, you will learn the most popular filters used by professionals. So, let us begin!

Using the Cross Star Filter

This is by far the most used filter among photography enthusiasts. The cross star filter can be used to create a star-like illusion out of light sources. Depending upon the cross star filter you have, the filter will turn the light source into a 4 point or 6 point star. Notice here that I am talking about the light source and not the light. If you look at a cross star filter, then you can easily see a pattern which is responsible for capturing the light source and for turning the same into a star. This filter is mainly used to add a little charm to the image without making it look fake. For the best results, I recommend using this filter when there are 3 or less light sources. This is because more light sources can distract the viewers. Or else, you can use it when the light sources are at an appreciable distance from each other.

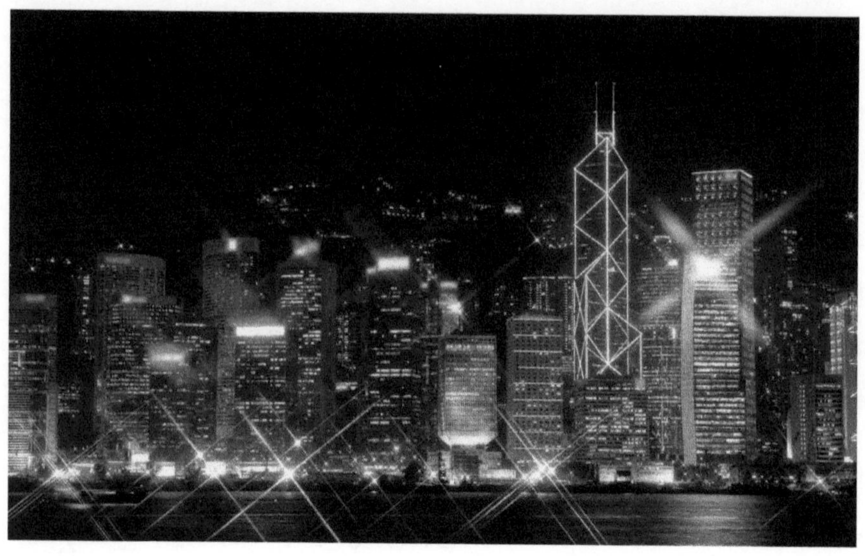

Using the Center Spot Filter

This is another popular filter used by professionals to play with focus. Although everyone likes to click the sharp images, there is a special place in photography for soft images as well. The images with soft parts are more artistically appealing. The Center Spot Filter is used to create softness at the edges of the image while keeping what's at the center of the image sharp. This filter is often used when your object is in the middle column of the rule of third. Using this filter allows the photographer to make a dreamlike artificial effect. Below is an example to help you understand this filter more clearly.

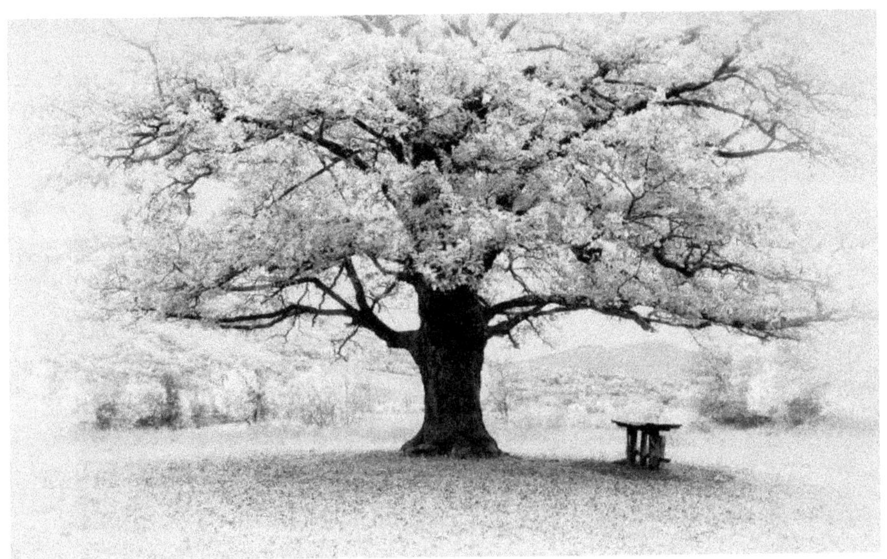

Using the Fog Filter

You can easily depict from the name itself that what this filter does. The fog filter adds fog as an artificial effect to your image. When you use the fog filter, the contrast of your camera is reduced which causes the incoming light to burst, hence creating a fog-like an effect in your images. This filter is often used to add a foggy morning effect in a landscape. You can also use this filter during the night. When doing so, the filter will make the stars appear bigger than their actual size and will help you in capturing their vivid colors. Filters are available in various intensities today: the 'A fog filter' has less fog intensity while the 'C fog filter' has high fog intensity. When using the fog filter, it is advised to adjust your aperture accordingly as the wide opening of the aperture can diminish the effect of the fog filters. Here is an example for you to see how this filter works.

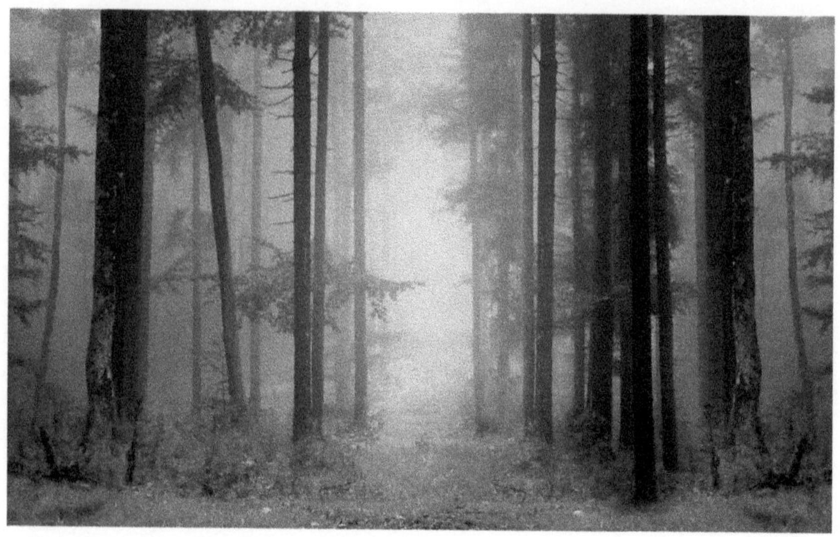

Using the Multi-Vision Filter

Cloning an object was a pain before, but today, with the help of multi-vision filter, you can easily multiply the object without any problem in your image. These filters are often circular in shape and are made up of two pieces. You can multiply the object from 2 to 6 times by rotating the first element of the multi-vision filter. This filter comes with 2 simple modes, namely circular and linear. In linear mode, the object will be multiplied in a straight line, while in circular mode, the same will be multiplied in a circular form.

Using the Infrared Filter

The infrared filter has always been in fashion for photography. Mainly because the infrared lights are not visible to the naked human eye. The camera, however, can easily see these infrared lights. The infrared filter is used by photographers to block any light which lies outside the infrared spectrum. This enables them to capture an image in a dramatic and smooth manner. Infrared filters are also known for increasing the contrast of the image which is impossible to achieve in any other filter. When you use infrared filters in your work, you are advised to use a long exposure time; this is because, in the infrared filter, most of the light is blocked, which can make your image look darker. Below is an image which was shot with the use of the infrared filter.

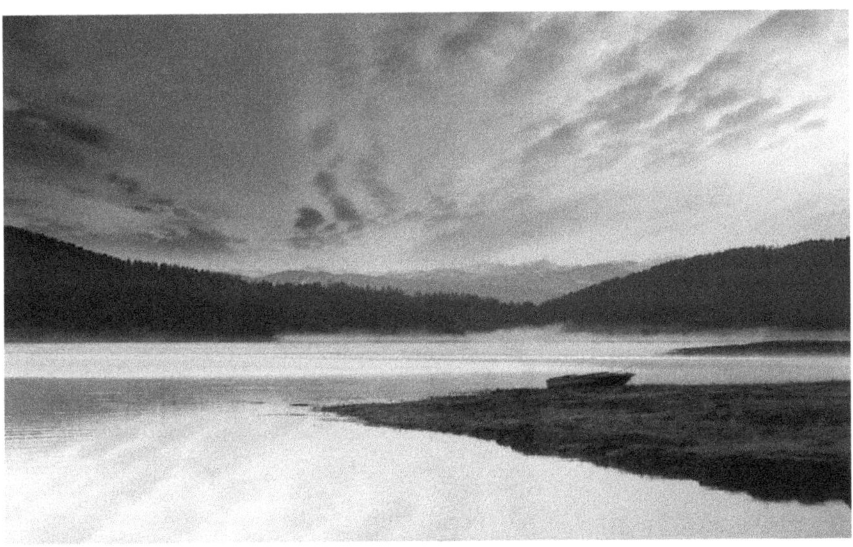

I hope you enjoyed the example images that I provided in this chapter to explain the various kinds of filters. You can always use a filter to make your image more appealing. If you do not want to use a filter, then you can easily use something like a candy wrapper to add an effect. Below is an example where the photographer used the pink candy wrapper to cover the bottom part of the lens to create a pinkish bottom for the image.

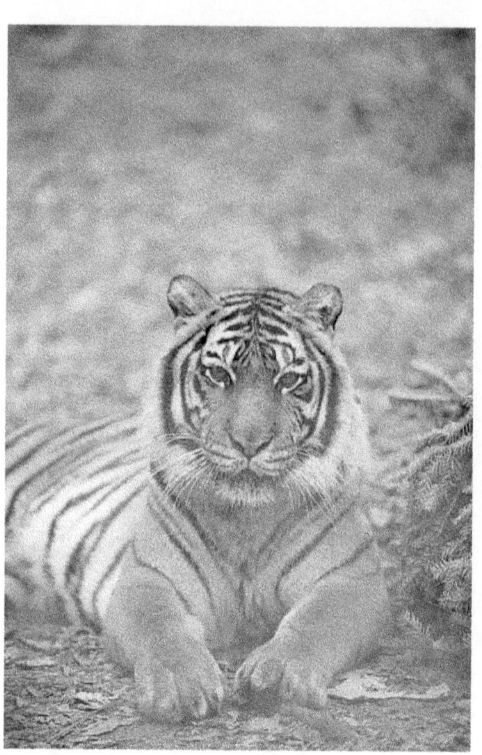

The End of a New Beginning

So, that's it with the photography lessons. If you have followed the book thoroughly till now, then you can easily see the improvements in your work. From now onwards, it is all about how passionate you are towards photography, and how much time you want to devote to practicing your skills. The more you practice, then better you will become at it. Now, we will start with the second part of this book, which is about Photoshop and how you can use it to create amazing images. Let us first start with the general introduction of Photoshop.

Introduction to Photoshop

Photoshop was launched in February 1990 and its launch entirely modified the manner in which digital pictures were handled. It caused a revolution within the world's artistic community and created a very easy method for everybody to edit pictures without forcing them to buy expensive equipment from the local stores. The revolution started with Photoshop in 1990 continues to be alive nowadays as well. There are many other image editing software programs available in the market like Paint.net, but still, Photoshop provides the simplest flexibility and freedom in modifying images the way a user wants to. This is the main reason why, even after competition with several companies for over twenty-two years, Adobe Photoshop continues to be the worldwide standard for each company to edit and build pictures.

Over the years, Adobe has added additional options to Photoshop, to make it more awesome than before. In this section of this book, you will learn the basics of Photoshop and how you can use this amazing piece of software to edit the images the way you want.

Understanding the Photoshop Screen

Before you can begin using Photoshop to edit the images, you need to understand how the Photoshop screen looks. It is important to know what lies where on the screen so that you can easily access everything that you want without wasting any time in finding them at the last moment. The Photoshop screen that you see once you start the software is known as the Photoshop Workspace. Although you can easily customize this workspace to fit your editing style, for the sake of keeping this book simple and easy for beginners, I will be explaining the default workspace that you see after opening the Photoshop. You will see various tools that Photoshop provides to its users for editing and creating purposes at the left side of the screen. The right side of the screen is mainly occupied with Photoshop panels. These panels have extra options for the tools you use and have various sections to help you keep the track of your work (layers and artboards). At the top of the screen, you have the menu bar from where you can access additional features like Transform, wrap, etc., which are not available from the left or right panels which are provided by default.

Below is a screenshot of the Photoshop workspace to help you understand it better.

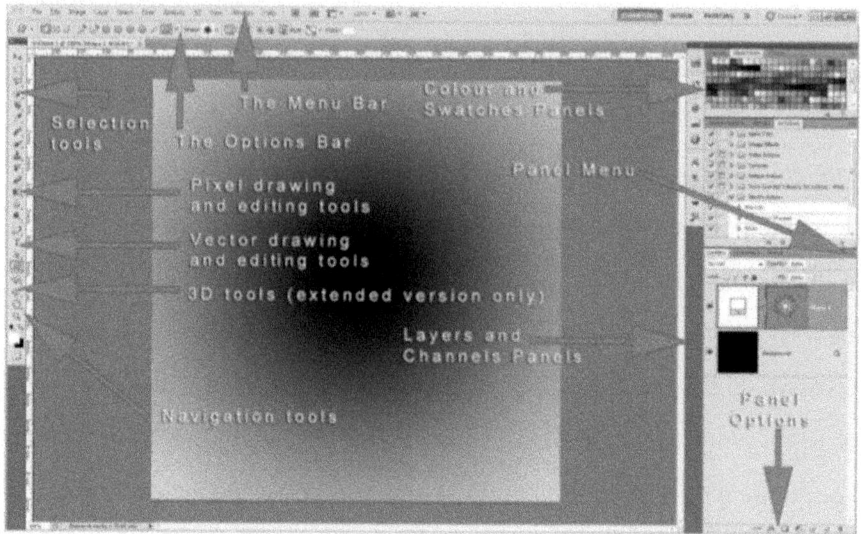

As you can see, both the left and right side tools and options are divided into various categories. For example, selection tools, navigation tools, layers, panels, color swatches, etc. Photoshop groups up the different tools according to their use to make it easy to remember where they are. This saves time in searching for tools in the Photoshop. In the next chapter of this book, you will learn about the toolbar, which provides various tools to the users for editing and creating purposes. Which will then be followed by the editing tutorials.

Understanding the Basic Photoshop Tools

All the basic Photoshop tools are provided in the toolbar section. Also known as the tool panel, this section is located on the left side of the Photoshop workspace by default. You can click and drag it to a new place if you want to. The toolbar section contains many mouse-based tools that a user can select while working in Photoshop for editing and navigating purposes. In the above workspace image, I have already named the various sections of tools that are present in this toolbar (like selection tools, navigating tools, etc.). If you look at the toolbar section closely, you can easily see that these sections are separated by a small line. The first group of tools is selection tools, which are followed by pixel editing tools, vector editing tools and navigation tools. After these sections, you will see a color picker at the bottom of the toolbar and an icon that allows you to enter the quick mask mode. This mask mode allows you to create selections for image editing. I have provided the burst view of the toolbar to help you understand about different groups and their respective tools.

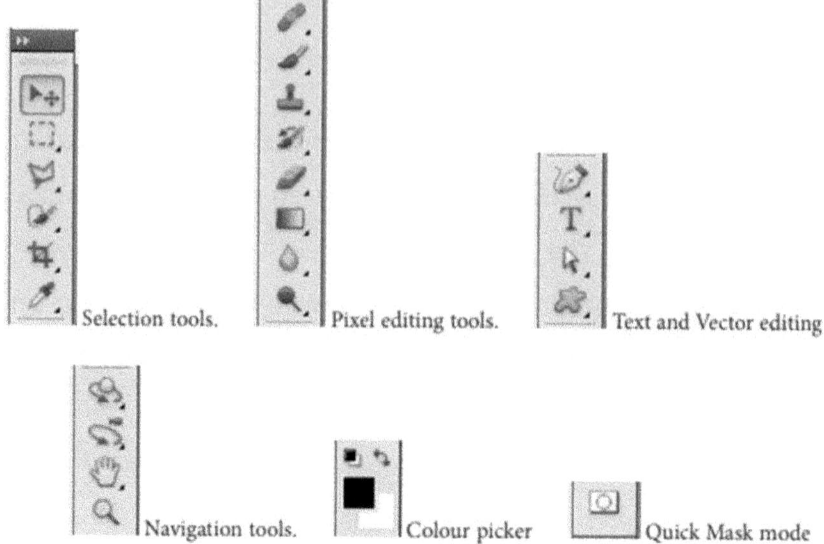

In the above image, you will notice that most of the tools have a small black arrow at the bottom right. Most beginners ignore this arrow icon. This icon actually means that there are more tools that can be accessed by the user by clicking and holding the tool. Once you do that, a list of extra tools will appear. Once the list appears on your screen, you can release the mouse and select the tool that you want to use; the list will remain until you make a selection or click anywhere else on the screen. An example of the extra tools list is shown in the image below.

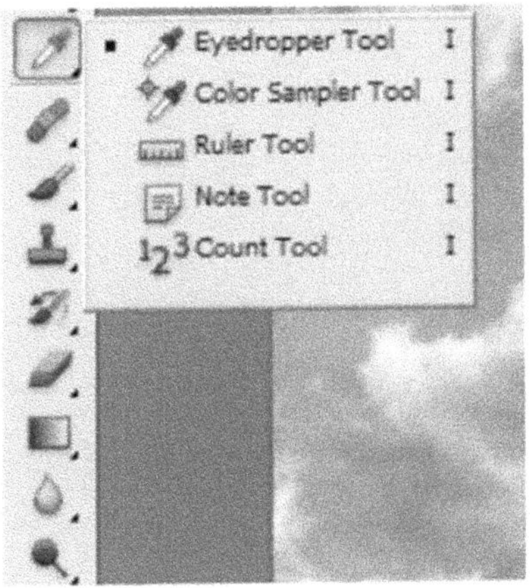

Now, let's learn about some of the most common tools used in Photoshop for editing purposes. It is recommended that you open these tools and try using them as you read about them for better understanding. This is the best way to learn about any software that you want to.

The Move Tool

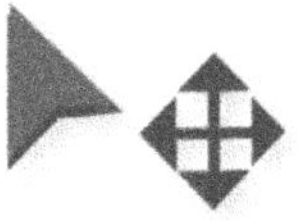

This is the most widely used tool in Photoshop or in any other image editing software available. You can move objects around the Photoshop workspace using the move tool. Click on the object to select it for moving, then click and drag to take it to its new position.

The Marquee Tool

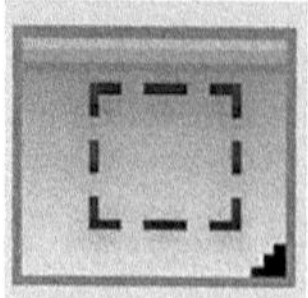

The next most widely used tool for editing purposes is the marquee tool. The user can select the canvas in a shape of this choice. A rectangular shape is a default, but the user can change to an ellipsis shape if needed.

The Lasso Tool

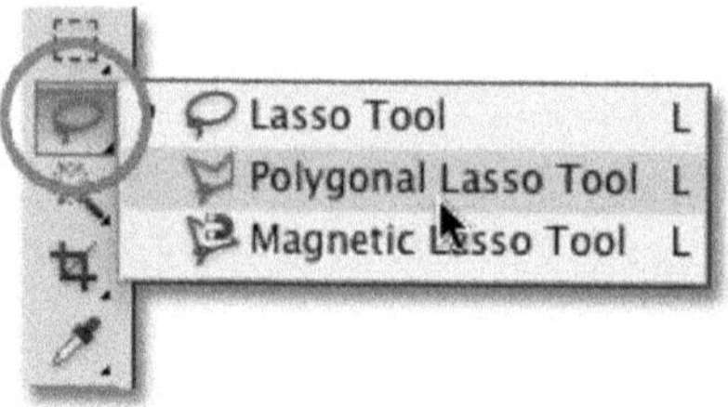

This is the tool which gets all beginners excited in Photoshop. Most users start selecting with Lasso Tool even in the case where a marquee tool can be used. The lasso tool lets you choose different parts of the canvas like a lasso, in a free-form manner. You can also select the polygonal lasso or a magnetic lasso tool from the extra tool list as shown in the image above. The magnetic lasso automatically detects edges for you.

The Magic Wand Tool

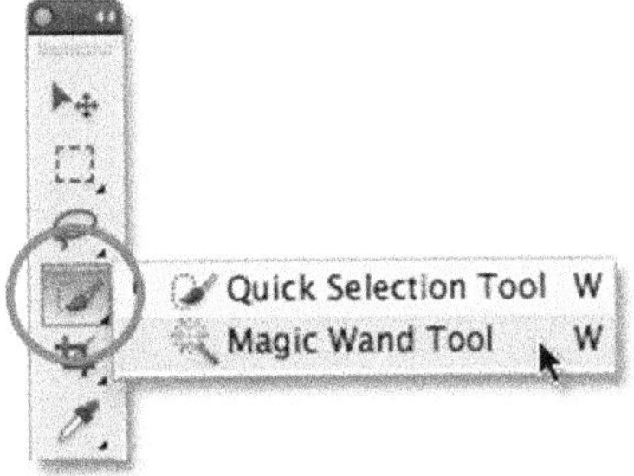

This tool makes selecting and editing easy when an area of similar color is to be selected quickly. This tool can be used as an 'out of the box' method to remove backgrounds from photos. Using this tool makes Photoshop select the spot that's selected and anything around it. However, this tool should not be used when you have very little difference in the color. For example, this tool will treat the white and light gray in the same manner. If you go to select the white object, it will automatically select the light gray as well.

The Crop Tool

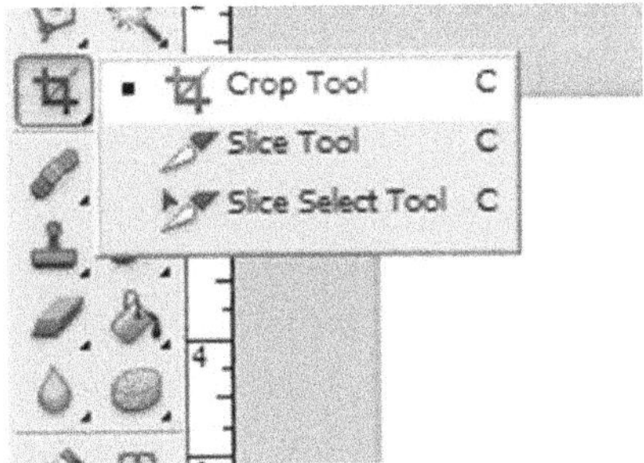

You must have used this tool on your smartphones. This tool is used to crop or cut a picture in Photoshop to any size that you wish.

The Eyedropper Tool

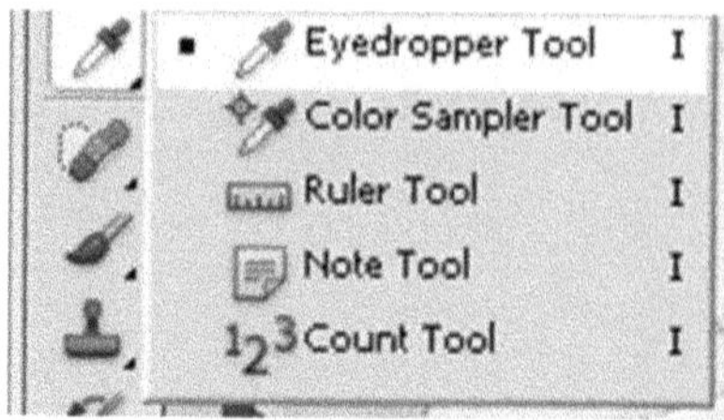

The Eyedropper lets you pick any color in your foreground or background as your selected color.

The Healing Brush Tool

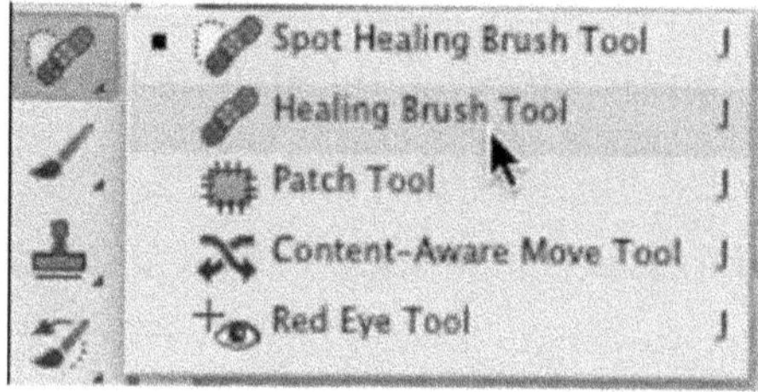

This is another famous tool for intermediate users of Photoshop. This lets you use part of the photograph to paint over another part. Photoshop will blend the surrounding areas of the picture as required.

Pencil and Paintbrush Tools

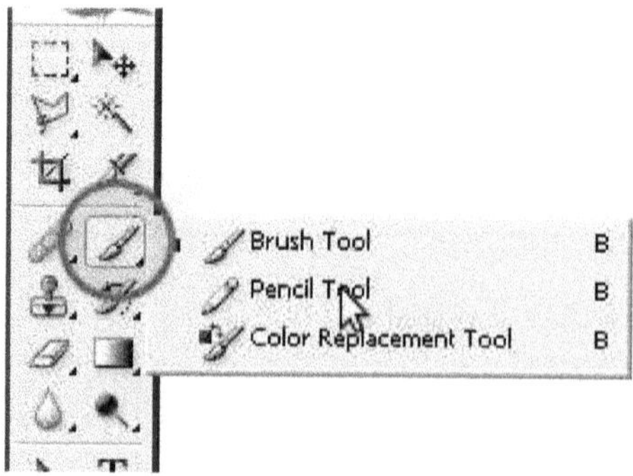

This is being used as a pencil. It can be adjusted to various sizes and shapes.

The Eraser Tool

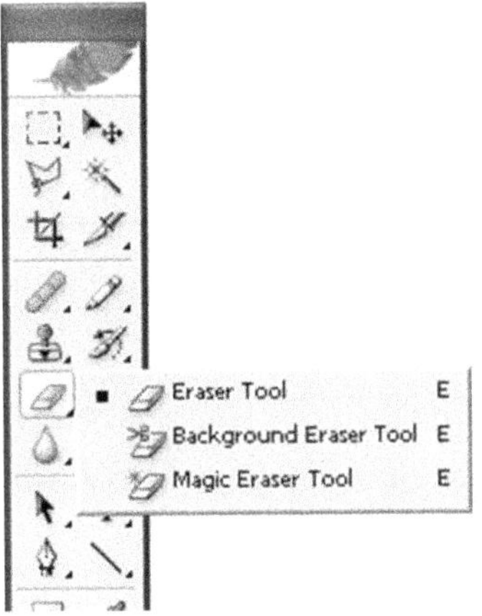

This is another tool that you must be familiar with because of the Paint application on your desktop or laptop. The eraser tool is almost identical to the paintbrush tool in Photoshop. The only difference is that it erases instead of painting a canvas.

The Paint Bucket & Gradient Tool

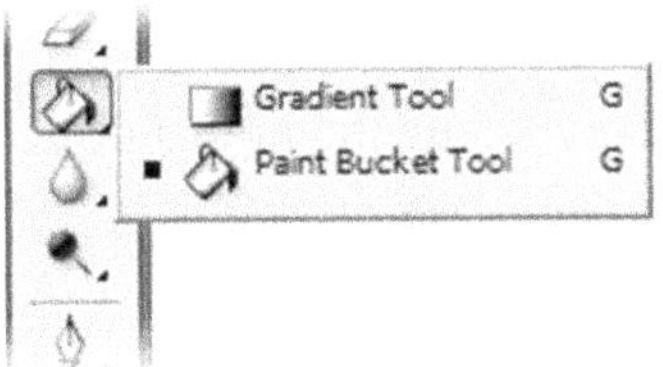

Again, the paint bucket is already known to you, but the gradient tool is a new term for you, right? I am going to explain both of them simultaneously, so you will understand better. The paint bucket tool works in a similar manner to the paint application and lets you fill it in with a certain foreground color. The gradient tool will blend the background with the foreground by creating a gradient. You can choose level and type of gradients required. These preset gradients are available in two or more colors which you can use.

The Pen Tool

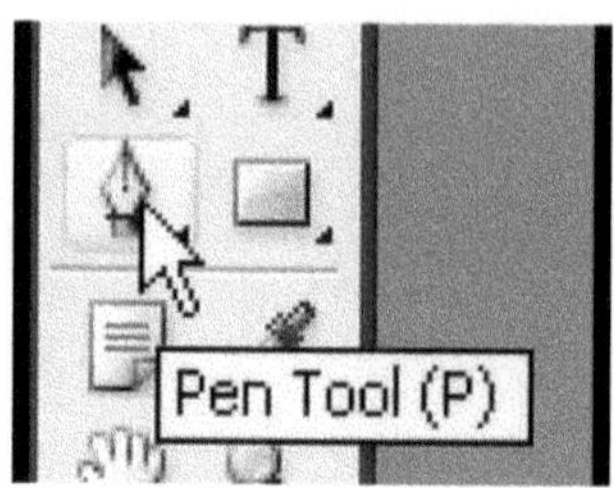

Suppose that the magic wand tool was of no help in changing the image's background because the background and image were very similar in color (like I said for the white and light gray color). In such cases, using a pen tool acts as a life saver for Photoshop users. Mastering the pen tool is the most challenging part for Photoshop beginners. But believe me, once you start using it, you will love it. As this tool is really important for Photoshop users, let's learn how to use it in detail.

To start with the Pen tool, open an image with a basic shape in Photoshop. Now, select the pen tool and click to create the edges of your shape. After completing it, you will see a little O if you hover over the first point. You can then click on that first point to close the shape. Hold ALT/OPT and click on a point to turn it from a curve to a straight line, and vice versa. It sounds really simple, doesn't it? But once you start using it, you will understand how much patience is required to master this small yet important tool.

The Text Tool

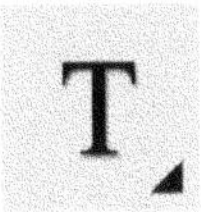

You must be familiar with this tool from the paint application on your desktop. However, the text tool is a little bit advanced in Photoshop. The text tool in Photoshop allows you to write in two different ways. It is really important that you understand both of these. The first way is how most people use text, by using what is called the Point text tool. You simply click on the Text Tool in the tools palette, click back on your image and start typing. The other way is to click on the Text Tool if it's not already clicked. Take the text tool and DRAG it out to make a rectangle. Now, you will be able to type in this rectangular box, and all the text that you type will be constrained by this box. This is known as Paragraph text. The paragraph text can be aligned in the box to the left, right, center or justify format as per your needs. One of the advantages of having a Photoshop CC version over Photoshop CS version is that CC support offers more fonts than CS version of Photoshop.

The Shape Tool

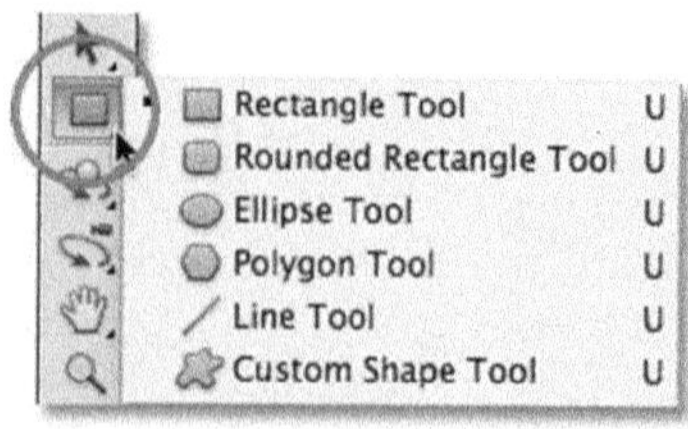

This tool makes creating simple shapes easy. With this tool, you can create rounded rectangles, vector rectangles, circles, polygons, custom shapes and lines. These shapes are very helpful when designing or creating shape masks for photos.

I hope that you have learned these tools by heart. Getting a good hold over these tools will help you in using Photoshop easily. Not only for editing the images but for creating new artworks as well. From the next chapter, we will begin our lessons on image editing as discussing every single basic aspect of Photoshop is beyond the scope of this book.

The Concept of Color Grading

Color grading is a process where the colors of an image are enhanced and altered to create visually appealing and dramatic work. This technique is applicable to all digital media: like images and videos. In fact, all the movies that you see and images that you like always go through color grading before being presented to the world in their final version. Color grading helps in correcting the color of the image and to add artistic effects to it. Below is an example of a screenshot from the movie House On The Pine Street, to show you how color grading actually works.

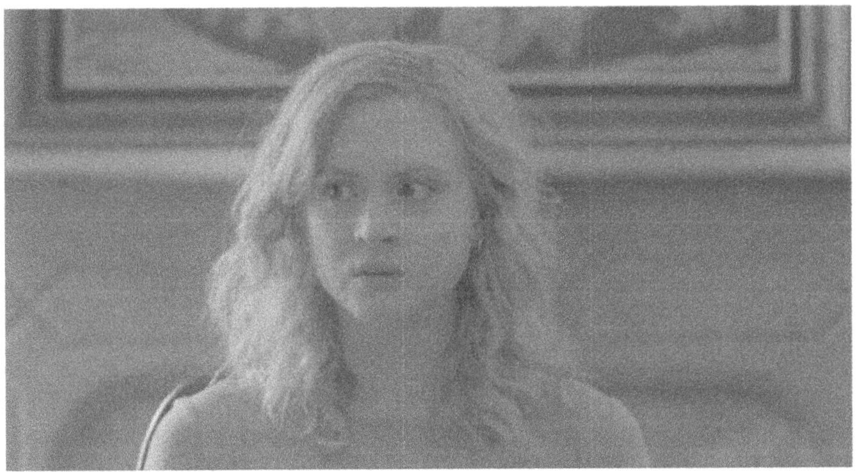

The image above is presented without any color grading. Now, look at the image provided below to see how amazingly the color grading alters an image.

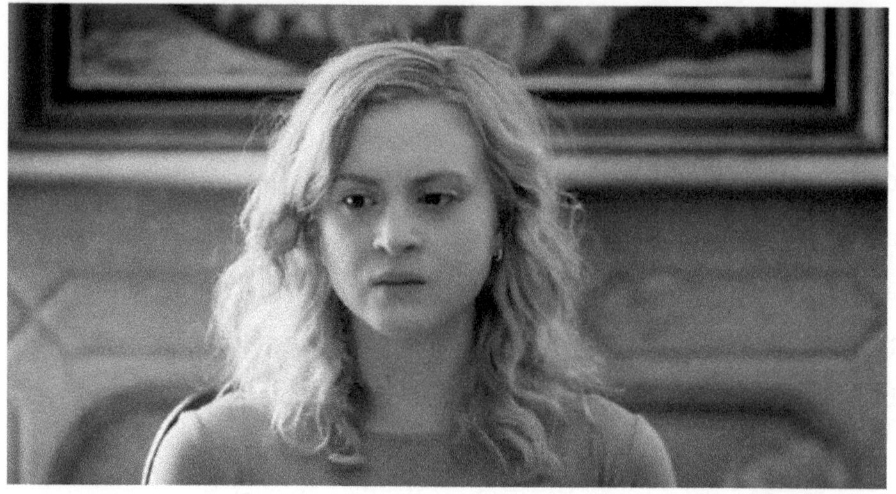

Did you see the difference? How amazing will it be if you can do this with the images yourself from your laptop? Well, that is possible, and it is exactly what I am going to teach you now.

The Color Grading Tutorial for Beginners

Okay, so before moving on, I want to tell you that to achieve good results in color grading you can use some settings in your camera to get the most stable images for this process. Below are some of the settings that I personally use in my camera while taking photos.

The Camera Settings for Color Grading

Always use a large aperture on your camera while taking photos. A value between f/1.4 and f/2.0 will do it. What we are trying to do here is to generate a bokeh effect, that is, blur what is in the background while having the things in the front stay sharp. I have already covered bokeh in the previous chapters of this book.

Light always plays an important role in the images. Having a shadow is often recommended rather than having a pale image of someone's face with no shadows. The shadows, however, need to be soft and not harsh. To achieve this, you can either use the artificial light, a flash diffuser (I have explained it already) or you can simply click the image immediately after sunset to get soft shadows.

These tips will always help you to capture the image in the most cinematic way possible, without any external help.

Now, let us learn how you can use color grading in Photoshop to enhance your images.

Color Grading in Photoshop

Color grading is done in Photoshop with the help of layers. Over the image, we keep adding several adjustment layers to apply the various effects. To those who are unfamiliar with layers, they are simply a collection of objects, or text, in Photoshop. When you place these layers one over the other, you get a full image. Here is an example –

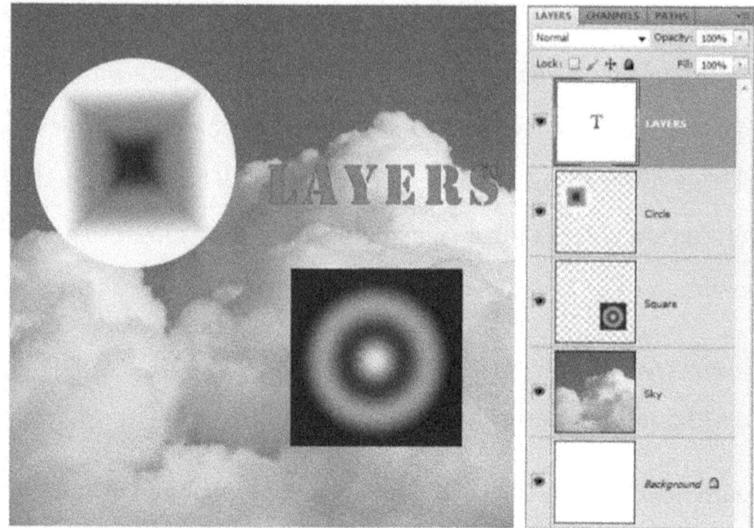

In the image above you can see that the full image is made up of 5 layers. Each layer can be individually edited to edit the image. The final result of the same is shown in the main Photoshop workspace. Now, let us move towards color grading. I am going to use the following image to teach you about the color grading process.

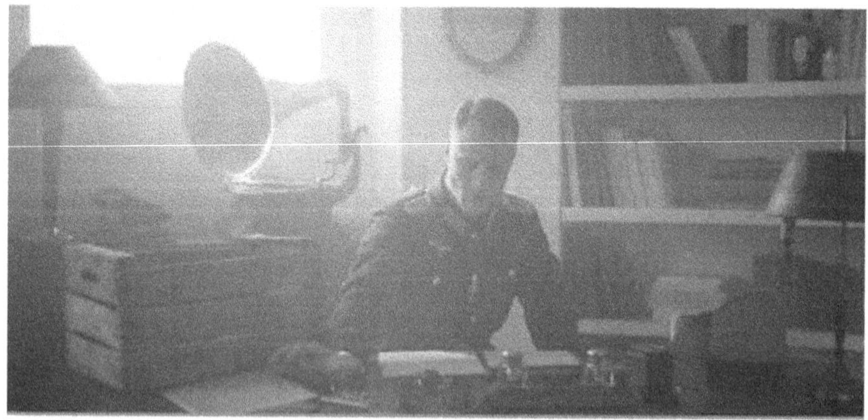

We will add color effects to this image by enhancing the yellow color in the highlights and green color in the shadows. So, let us begin!

Firstly, open the image in the photoshop, it will be shown with the name – background, with a lock sign over it. Now, you need to right-click on this layer and select the option which says 'duplicate the layer'. This will make a copy of the image which you can edit. This is done so that you can preserve the original image in case you don't like the editing that you did on its copy. You can then use the original image to make a new copy to begin editing.

We will now add an adjustment layer to this image. To do so, go to the menu bar and click on layers, then select the new adjustment layer. A new side list of commands will open in front of you, from here, select the Color LookUp option as shown in the image below.

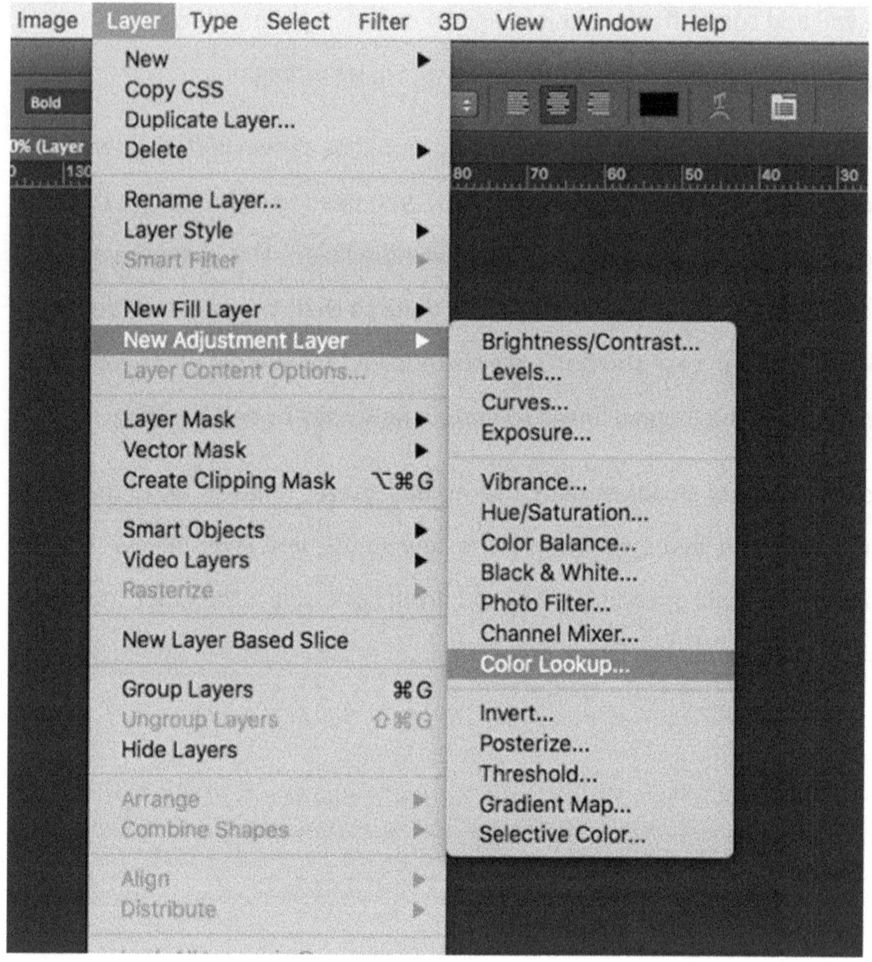

A new dialogue box will appear in front of you to enter the layer name, you can enter whatever you like. To keep track, I usually use the Color Look Up to remember what this layer is doing. Below the name field, you will see the opacity option. I recommend using 20% as the opacity value for the work. Otherwise, the effects that you will add will be too strong. After adjusting the opacity, all you need to do is to hit enter to add this layer. Now, open the layer properties for editing. To do so, you can right click on the color look up layer and select edit adjustment. Now, for the 3DLUT file option, select filmstock_50.3dl.

Now, the next step is to enhance the image with the help of curves adjustments. To do this, add a new curve adjustment layer. Go to layers -> New Adjustment Layer and then select curves. For the use of curves, you can keep the opacity to 100% so that they can redo the contrast of the image properly. After adding the curves layer, open the properties and you will see a graph with a curve from bottom left to the top right corner. How much contrast you want in your image depends on you, and you are free to adjust it according to your needs.

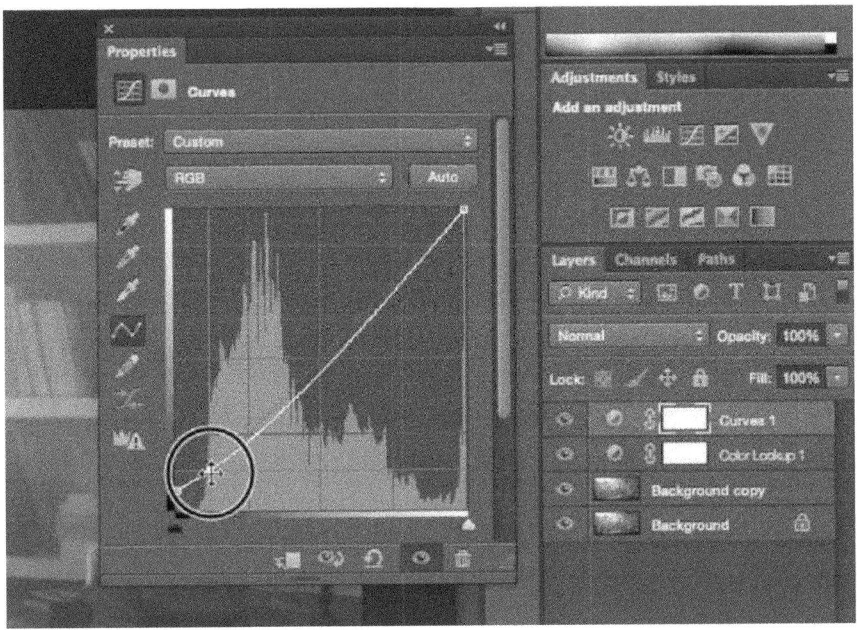

After adjusting the contrast, we will add another curves adjustment layer with 100% opacity. In the properties of this new layer, instead of RGB, select blue. Now, lower the curve end from the top right corner as shown in the image below.

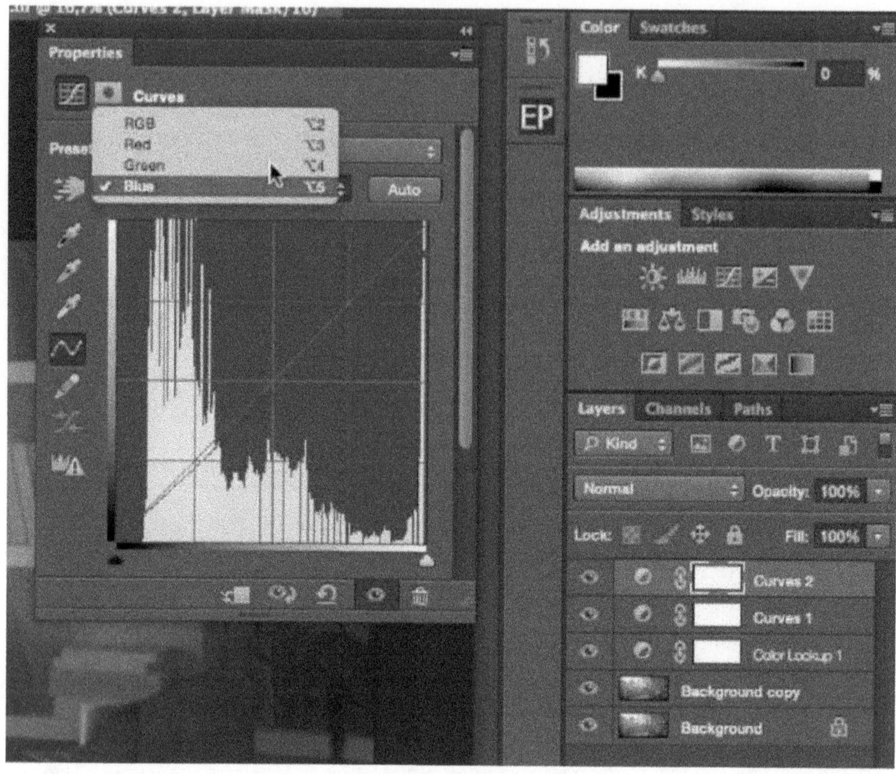

Doing so will add a yellow effect to the shadows present in your image. Once you are done with the adjustment according to your needs, you can proceed to add another adjustment layer with 100% opacity to adjust the overall color balance. To do so, you will need a color balance layer. Go to layers -> New Adjustment Layer and select the color balance. Open its properties to balance the yellow and green to add effects to your image. Here is what your screen will look like once you open the properties –

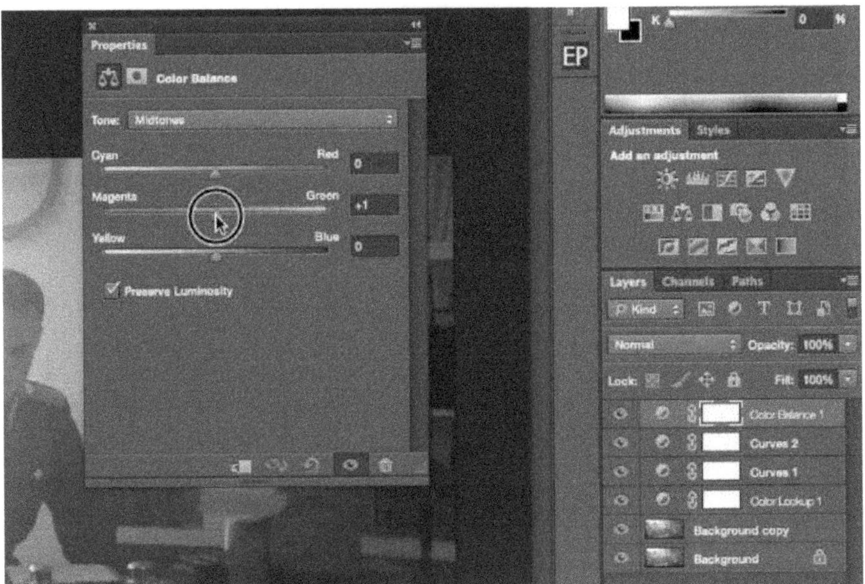

In the tone tab, select Midtones and change the amount of green color in your image. This will enhance the shadows of your image. Now, from the tone option, select the Highlights and adjust the yellow color to enhance the light in your image as shown in the image below.

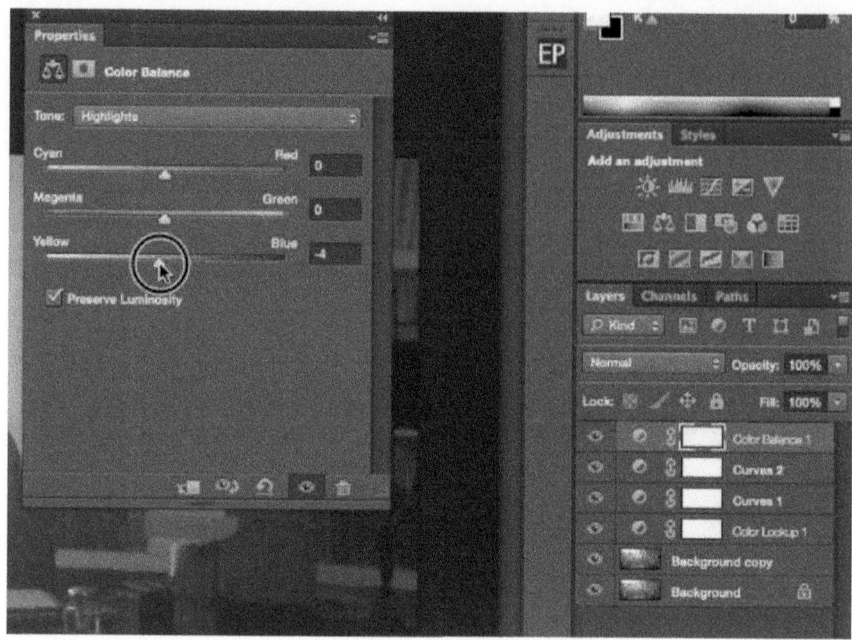

Now, let us lighten up the image a little. To do so, add another curves layer with 100% opacity and adjust the graph for RGB to increase the amount of light in your image. In case you want to darken your image, you can follow the same, but instead of taking the curve towards up to add light, you will have to take it towards the bottom to darken the image. You can add these two images with the separate opacity to make an advanced effect on your image.

After doing all the steps, here is what my image looks like. In the next chapter, we will learn what photo manipulation is and how we can combine the two images to create a single cool-looking picture.

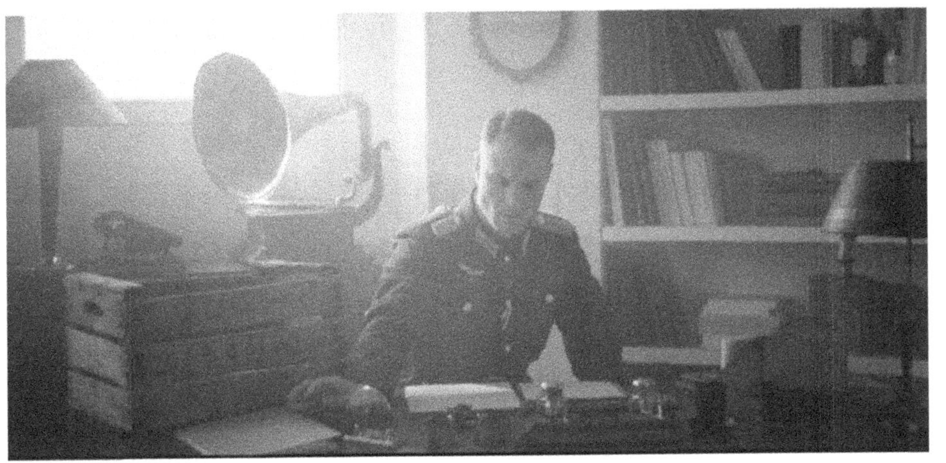

Photo Manipulation

Photo manipulation is nothing but another effective technique which is used by professionals for creating amazing images. It is a process which involves various operations (example color grading) to add the desired changes to the photographs. Photo manipulation is widely used today for works included in advertisements, promotions, magazines, artworks, etc. In professional language, it is known as retouching the images to enhance their visual appearance. One of the most used photo manipulation techniques is to combine the two images to make an amazing picture. Let us see how it is done.

Let us combine the following two images to create a cool looking picture.

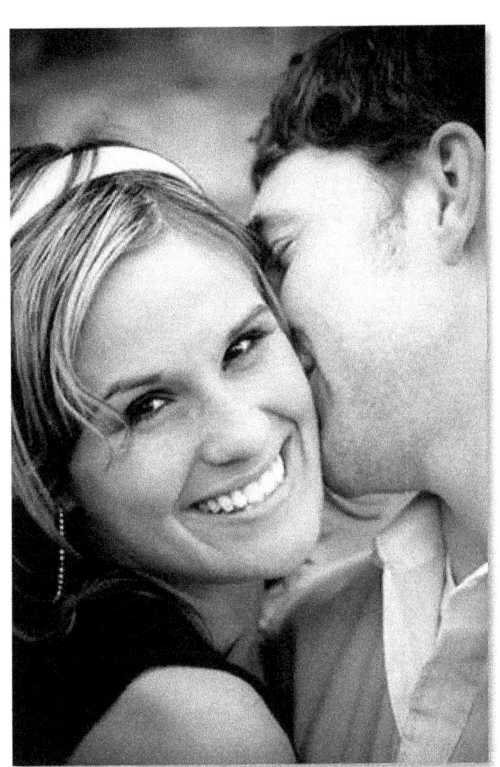

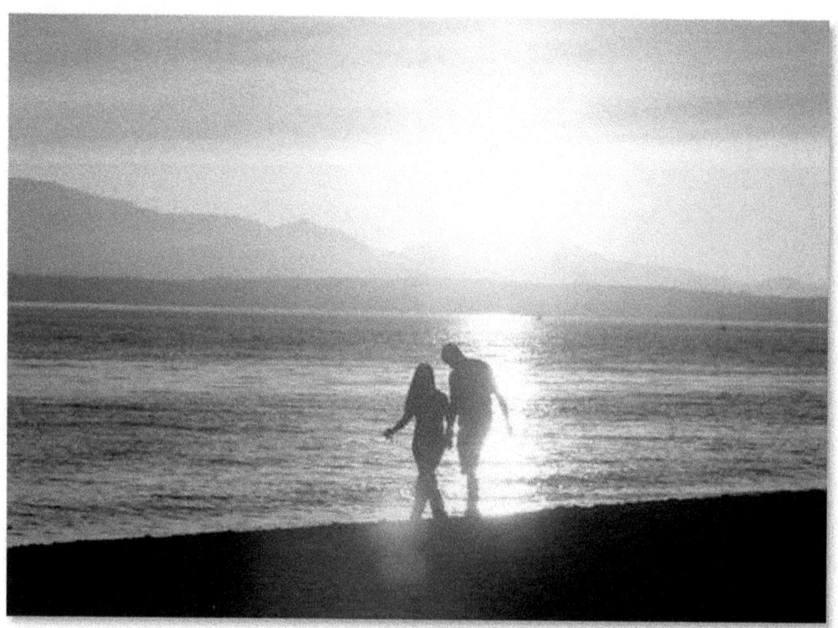

Now, start by opening the first file in Photoshop. To edit the image, right click on the layer named background in the Photoshop layers panel and then select 'convert to smart object' as shown in the image below.

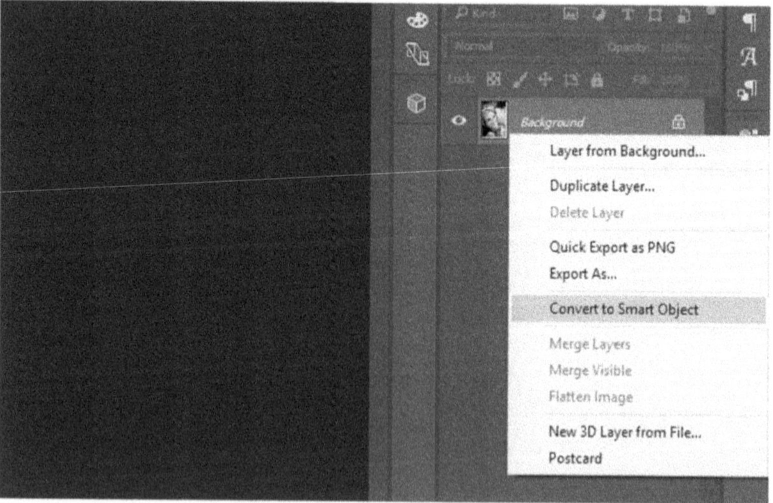

Now, add the second image file to the first file. You can simply drag the second image from the file explorer and release it in Photoshop over the first image. It will look something like the screenshot below –

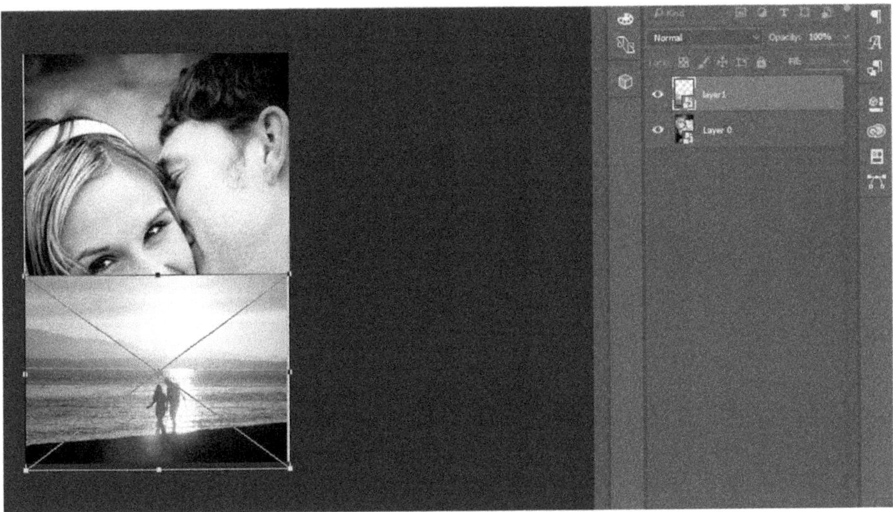

Now, hit enter to place the image there. Once you place the image, you can use the move tool to get the image to the bottom, as shown in the screenshot above. Now, hit the Ctrl+T from your keyboard to launch the free transform tool. Now, resize the bottom image so that its width is as much as the width of the first image, as shown in the screenshot below.

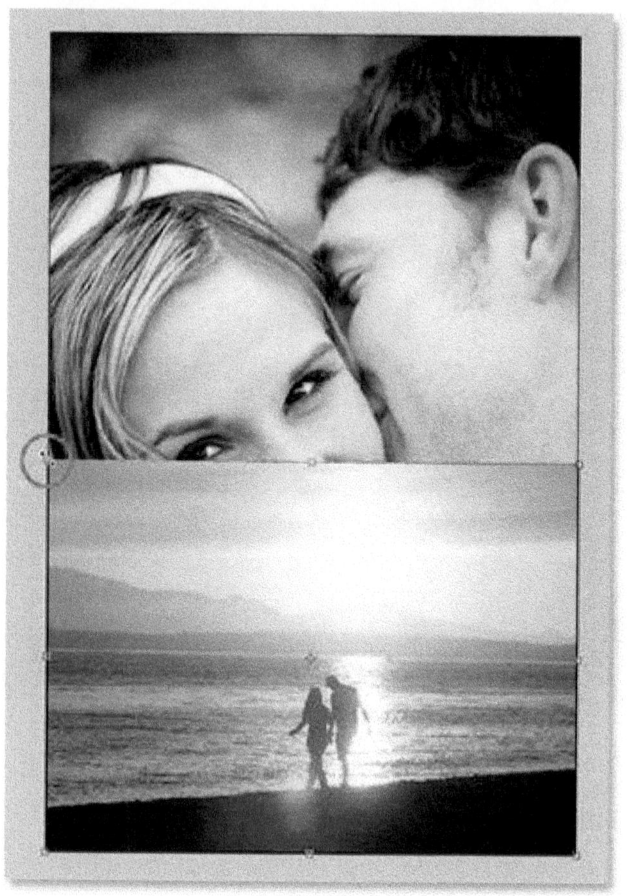

Now, we will use the same free transform technique on the first image to change its position. To make sure that you do not alter the image height to width ratio accidently, and that you move it in a straight line, I recommend that you hold the shift key while operating.

So, hold the shift key and move the image a little higher to get the results shown in the screenshot below.

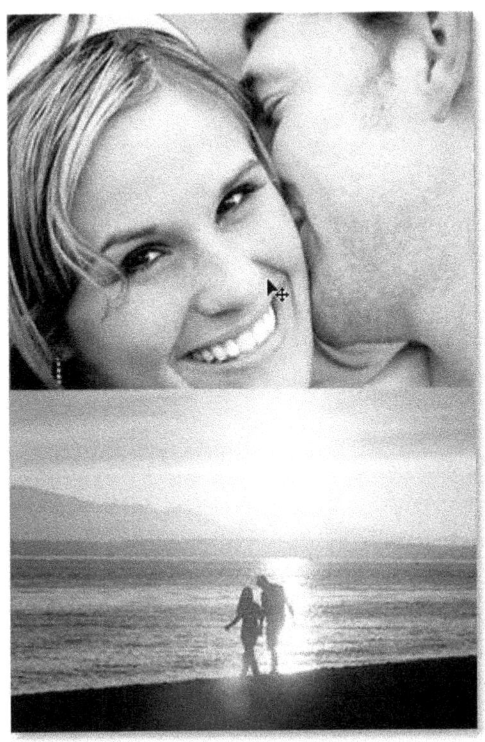

Here you can see that the face of the woman is fully visible now, whereas the man's hair is not. The point here is to get what matters from the image inside the working frame so that it is completely visible. For me, the face of the woman was more important than the man's hair.

The next thing that you need to do is to create a layer mask over the second image (that I, the one with the sunset). To do so, select the marquee tool with the second image layer set as active, then select the whole image. Now, go to layers -> Layer mask and click reveal all. You will now see an additional layer has been linked to the layer of the second image, as shown in the screenshot below –

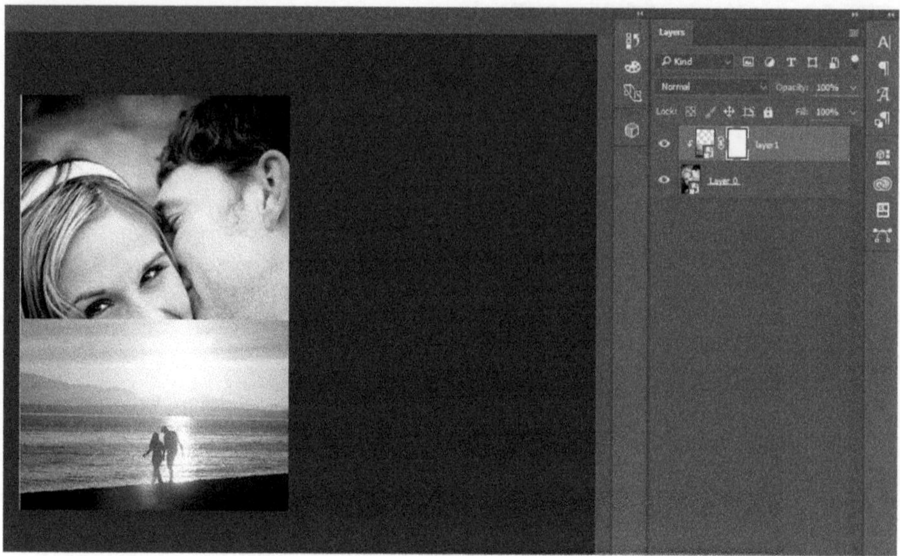

Note here that the layer mask is shown with the white background with a border around it. If you do not see anything like that and see just a white background without border, it means that you have linked a layer and not a layer mask. You should only and only link the layer mask.

Now, let us start blending the two images with the help of this layer mask. From the toolbar, select the gradient tool and then from the options bar, which is just below the menu bar at the top of your screen, select the black to white gradient. Below is an image to help you out on this –

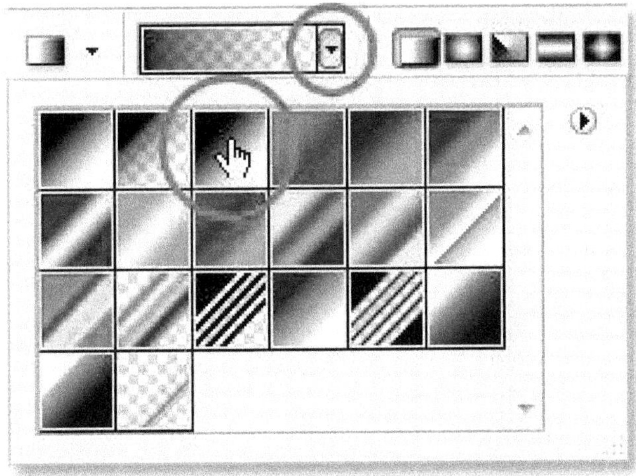

Now, click anywhere else on the screen (not on the image) to close the options. Now, go back to the image, select the layer of the second image linked with a layer mask. And then, holding the shift button on your keyboard, click and drag along a line on the second image, as shown in the image below –

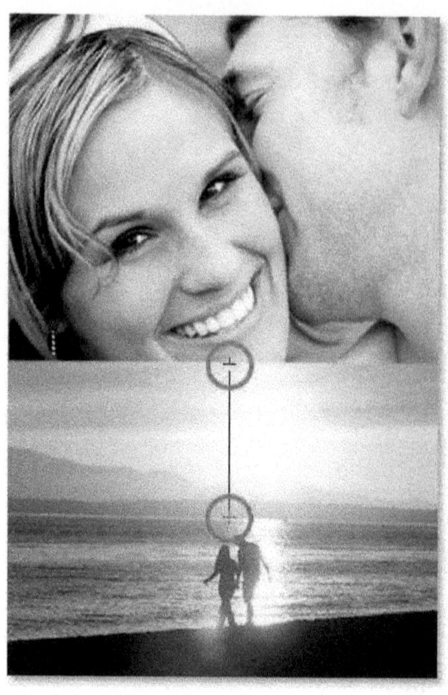

Once you reach the bottom end of the line, release the mouse to apply the gradient effect to your image. It will look similar to the screenshot shown below –

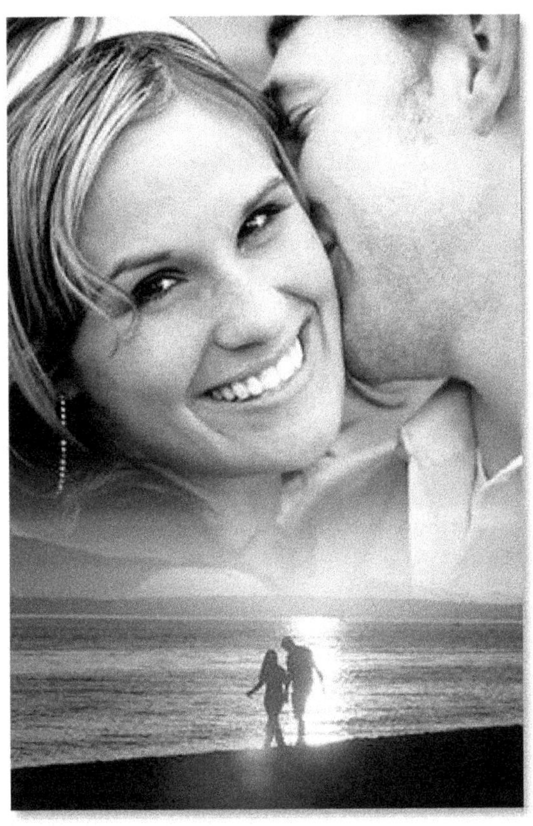

Now, we are done with the combining and editing part of the image. Now we can merge these two layers together to create a single image out of them. To do so, select the two layers from the layers panel and then right click and select – Merge Layers. Photoshop will now create a new layer for this purpose. Now, we can continue to add the color of our choice to this image. To do so, we will first have to desaturate the image to change it to black and white. To remove all the color from your image hit Ctrl+Shift+U from your keyboard. You will now see a desaturated image like the screenshot below.

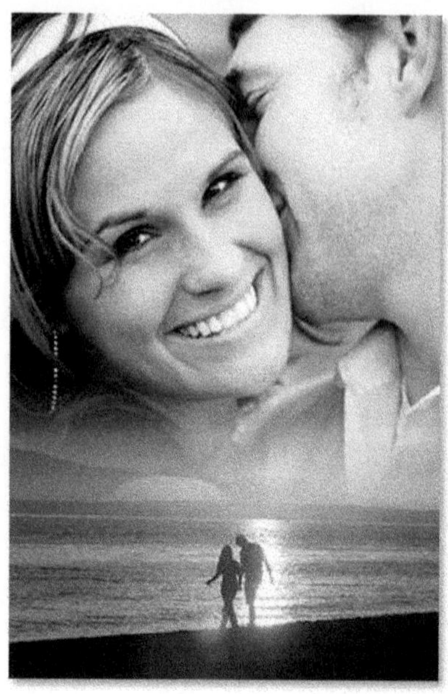

Now, you can add a new color layer to add a color of your choice. To do so, go to layers -> New Fill Layer and then select the Solid Color option. As soon as you do this, you will be provided with the color dialogue to select the solid color for your image. I selected the purple color, and the results of this action are shown below –

You can see that my whole image was covered with the purple color. Now comes the interesting part. Now, we will change the blend mode of the color layer from Normal to something else. In the screenshot below, I changed the blend mode to screen from normal –

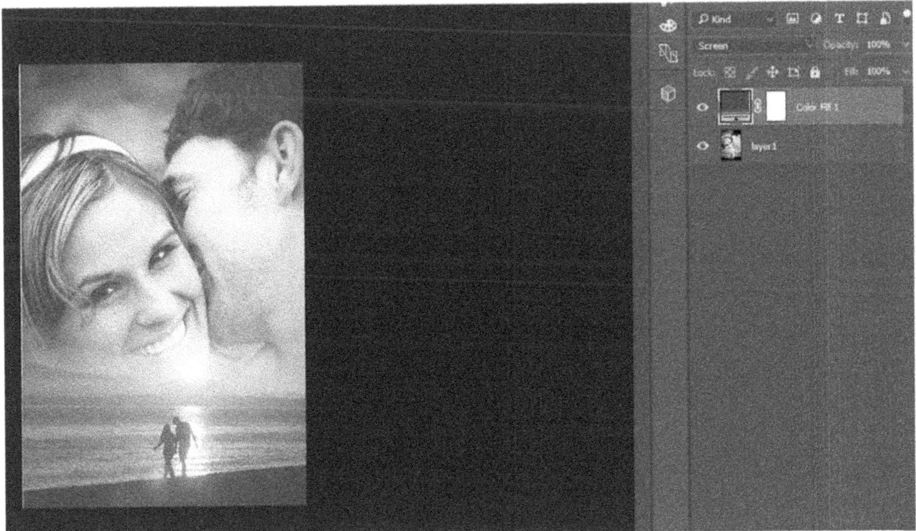

For the same layer, I changed the blend mode from screen to subtract to get a cool greenish effect on my image. Here is a screenshot to help you understand –

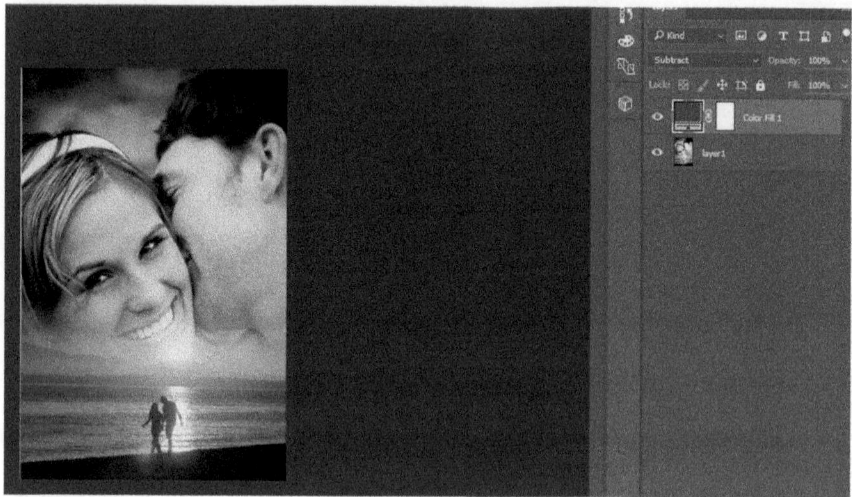

With this, we have reached the end of the chapter on photo manipulation and how to combine the two images to create a single cool image. I hope that this chapter was useful for you.

Conclusion

So, we have come to the end of my book on Photography and Photoshop. I hope that you enjoyed it and learned a lot from it at the same time. Like anything else, both Photography and Photoshop require time. The more time you give to them, the faster you will improve your skills. Finally, I again want to thank you for purchasing this book. I have done my part, and now it's your turn. So, get started with Photography and create some amazing images out of the pictures that you capture.

Good Luck!

www.ingramcontent.com/pod-product-compliance
Ingram Content Group UK Ltd.
Pitfield, Milton Keynes, MK11 3LW, UK
UKHW020235250726
13967UKWH00001B/375